D1448647

MODER DY

Mother Wave

MODER DY

Mother Wave

Roseanne Watt

First published in Great Britain in 2019 by
Polygon, an imprint of Birlinn Limited

Birlinn Limited
West Newington House
10 Newington Road
Edinburgh EH9 1QS

9 8 7 6 5 4 3 2

www.polygonbooks.co.uk

ISBN 978 1 84697 487 8

British Library Cataloguing-in-Publication Data
A catalogue record for this book is available
from the British Library.

The publisher gratefully acknowledges investment from
Creative Scotland towards the publication of this book.

Typeset in Verdigris MVB by Polygon, Edinburgh
Printed and bound by Bell & Bain Limited, Glasgow

for Alexandra Watt
(the original kishie wife)

'The old Shetland fishermen still speak with something like reverence of the forgotten art of steering by the moder dai (mother wave), the name given to an underswell which it is said always travels in the direction of land no matter from what airt the wind may blow, and even in the calmest weather.'

SCOTS MAGAZINE (November, 1949)

CONTENTS

KOKKEL

A NOTE TO THE READER

A few of the poems in these pages are written in the local vernacular of the Shetland Islands. Shaetlan, as locals have named it, is a form of Scots shaped by sea roads. It forms something of a fraught coalition between English, Lowland Scots and old Norn: the extinct Scandinavian language of the Northern Isles. This Norse element is retained mainly in the speech patterns and grammar of the dialect, as well as in place-names, and words which describe the natural world.

Shaetlan has no standardised orthography. Spelling is entirely dependent on a speaker's preference, and often dictated by their own local accent, which can vary quite drastically from island to island. This will perhaps lead to some confusion over the pronunciation of 'moder dy' – especially given the difference in spelling between this collection's title and its epigraph. I chose this particular spelling of the title because it was the one which I encountered most frequently in descriptions of the phenomenon. The epigraph, however, renders its spelling in a much more phonetic manner. To be clear, then: 'dy' is pronounced like the English word 'die', and not 'dee' (which is, funnily enough, the Shaetlan way of saying the word 'die').

On a sonic level, Shaetlan reflects its landscape; hard and open, yet with constant fluctuations of light. I like this wilderness inside it; the way it occupies a poem's heart. With all this in mind, though I have provided some 'uneasy translations' for these dialect poems, I have also not striven to replicate their verse all too faithfully in English. For a truer understanding of these poems, I hope you'll look to the supplied glossary, where each word can be read and measured with the full weight of its meaning behind it.

When I was very young, I could not 'hear' certain aspects of the dialect which my Shetland relatives spoke. I suppose you could attribute this to the fact that my father spoke Shaetlan, whilst my mother spoke English with an Irish cadence. These two forms of speech were of equal weight in my mind, and I could discern no stark differences between them. As well as this, I was too young to know which words were indeed dialect words; 'peeriewyes' (gently), 'spaegie' (aching muscles after physical exertion), 'essy-kert' (the bin lorry), 'skorie' (a young gull) – these were, once upon a time, just words to me.

I don't remember what this state of mind was actually like to live within; I can only recall the moment it ended. It was shortly after I started school, and I had been speaking on the phone to my grandmother. Over the crackling landline, I suddenly heard her saying 'du' instead of you, 'de' instead 'the'. From that point forward, it was as though both English and dialect had bifurcated in my mind. And with this, a choice seemed to present itself: *which one?*

nu yurden du art fur afyurden du viːs skæʔd oktoa

Aert du is
fir o aert du wis made
hame-trowe tae aert

*

Earth you are
for of earth you were made
return now to earth

STOAL (N)
An old story or legend.
[Orig. obsolete]

HAEGRI
for Stuart

The day you mapped your bonhogas
out for me, we saw it
curled like a question mark
at the lip of the hill –

and we'd thought it was a trick
of slud-light and lisks
before its unfolding into air,
as though hearing a call

above the swollen burn
you'd named *The Waterfall*,
beyond *The Flumes, The Secret Beach*,
the white stacked stones

of old stories we wish to find
some truth in. Haegri,
hillside-sentinel, what took you
from those blackened pools

you've spent lifespans watching over,
as though you were looking
for the image of some other
world within your own –

haegri, what voice summoned you
from your post, abandoning
these places we have not yet
quite returned from.

LICHEN LEID

symbiosis

what language is this
written on the stones
it looks like a petri dish

parasite

o blue-finskit tongues
shaipit lik skerries
i de flesh o de rock

TATTIEBOKEY
Innadaeks

Come you to the krub, and I
will axe you   to tread light

upon the skröf of things.   Here
the ground is thin

as milk,   restless as a cradle.
It's not yours to take.

This aert has no roots,
no seeds, despite the stones'

mimicry. The only tree
is my own cross;

even the crows know this.
Take vaar if they come.

They'll want the gludderi fruit of your eyes,
the perfect pips of your pupils.

I wonder what they'd sprout
if set in soil?

Not apple, olive, ash.
You would not bud.

There's something in the seams of you
suggesting   oat

or even
straw.

Yes. You'd come up
with your arms reksed out.

For three whole seasons
your mouth would gru   like this.

KISHIE WIFE
Ootadaeks

Though some say otherwise,
she was the first
who went to fetch the fire
from the hills. Of course she was.
No one else could bear
a load like that, slung over her back
like an infant; all its brilliant,
burning weight.

HAAFMAN

Him, the keeper of language, holds
up the blue harp of a porpoise jaw
for the wind to pluck at.

In the light of the lomm,
the mackerelled marble of his eye
                            glinks

SPEAKING SHAETLAN

Here's the trick:
pretend your mouth is full
               of stones.

Feel the dead weight
          pressing
on your tongue,

the way this opens
         your throat, turning your mouth

into a cave,
      a wide darkness.

Then (and this is crucial)
         let them
        drop

still spit-warm from your lips
and watch

how they could shatter
on impact

        anything
        which they struck,
        how they could break

        like bone,
           or bread.

SAAT I DE BLÖD

Lass, du's parched dy tongue
o dy ain laand. Knappit
dy wirds sae dry dey sift
atween dy teeth lik saand
sprittin doon an ooerglass.
I gied dee a langwich, wan
dat cud captir de percussion
o waves apo its consonants,
unravel de treads o de sowl
wi a single wird: shoormal,
mareel, bonhoga; a gift
dat du's left oot tae mulder
i de rees.

Lit me start ower:
Lass, du dösna hae de wirds
tae haad me on de page,
an du'll nivir fin me dere
until du understaands
de saat dat coorses trowe
dy veins is de lifeblöd
o an aulder converseeshun,
wan dat ebbs and flodds
joost as de tide. Dese wirds
ir my hansel tae dee.
Tak dem; gie dem
                    a pulse

SALT IN THE BLOOD

Lass, you've parched your tongue of your own land.
'Propered' your words so dry they sift between
your teeth like sand flitting down an hourglass.
I gave you a language, one that could capture
the percussion of waves on its consonants,
unravel the threads of the soul with a single word:
shoormal, mareel, bonhonga;
a gift that you've left out to moulder in the gales.

Let me start over:
Lass, you don't have the words to hold me
on the page, and you'll never find me there
until you understand the salt that courses
through your veins is the lifeblood
of an older conversation, one that ebbs and floods
just as the tide. These words are my gift to you.
Take them; give them a pulse.

THE DOORS

I woke

to feathered light

    your face

        smiling down

you called me

        Good Morning

    lifted me

      into the day

    where I would discover

        the doors of our house

          all the rooms

          they opened on

FLEDGLING

We found it on the dappled path
to primary school: a sparrow
fledged too early from the nest.

You stopped and stooped
and cupped it in your palms
with such a gentleness

I'd not seen in you before –
as though it were a windswept heart
made manifest; feather light

and hollow, a weight
like nothing in your hand – yet,
a whole life depended on it.

NESTING FAERIE RING

you open mouth
you ring of teeth

softly bared to show
things better kept

below.

THE MOON JELLYFISH

We find them melting
by the shoormal, like dropped

scoops of translucent ice-cream,
the same morning

of the old fisherman's funeral
at the chapel by our beach.

We'd seen the coffin going past
in a parade as slow as shadows

cast by summer clouds,
into the churchyard where

blind headstones watched us
playing daily with the waves.

The beach is filled with dead things.
Except the jellyfish.

We know they are immortal,
so when storms bring them

to the shore it is the saddest sight –
at least, that's what the fisherman

said. We want to save
the jellyfish. They ooze

between our fingers as we wade
out to the shallows, toss each

into the softly crooning waves.
Some have purple crescent moons

inside them; we think
they are the girls.

We do not know
the jellyfish are folklore,

a myth we're offering
the tide to be rejected:

for the dead will continue
being dead.

No; we know only the morning
deepening in the spaces

between pebbles, and the jellyfish
returning, dream-like, to shore.

SJUSAMILLABAKKA (N)

Between the sea and the shore

[O.N. *sjór*: the sea + *milla*: between + *bakki*:
shore, riverbank]

STEEPEL

It doubtless was / a holy thing / to see them there,
the ling, lying open / on the stones, / unfolded
from the thick / books of their bodies, / pining for
that hallowed / bloom of salt; / the haafmen still
there, too, / on the ayre, / stacking, unstacking
and restacking them / into a structure built / not
for reaching heaven / but as a tome / to keep their
summer in; / its sacred texts / of sun, sea and wind

RAAGA TREE

Da sie's da wye da wirld kums tae wis

Robert Alan Jamieson

Ta see me
is ta see

a vodd
wirld, shakkeld

atween tang
an auld nets.

Du winna
fin me dere –

no as I
wance wis.

See, I wis
browt here

by rees,
de sea-vaege

made me uncan;
made swart

taentacles
o my röts,

RAAGA TREE

To see me is to see
an absent world
caught between
seaweed and old nets.
You will not
find me there –
not as I once was.
See, I was
brought here
by storms,
the sea voyage
made me strange;
made black tentacles
of my roots,

twarterit
my boady

wi de grün
o thunderbolts.

Whit I wis
I hardly

mind mysel.
Dunna axe me.

Laeve me.
I hae no time

fir dy wilt göds.
My boughs

sanna be
gallows here.

crossgrained my body
with the green
of sharp porphyry.
What I was
I hardly remember.
Don't ask me.
Leave me.
I have no time
for your lost gods.
My boughs shall not
be gallows here.

TIRRICK SKULL

Noo du is nae mair
as pipper bon, töm

sockets stoorin
at de wind's erts,

dem gaets o air
du put by in de hadd

o dy mindin;
noo, weet saand

is aa de bruks o maettir
dat wance granted

dee dy bu
o lift

ARCTIC TERN SKULL

now you are no more
than paper bone,
empty sockets glowering
at the wind's directions,
those paths of air
you stored in memory's nest;
now wet sand is all
that remains of matter
which granted you
your house of sky

THE OIL RIGS

Do you mind them?
         The floating fairgrounds
of their bodies, which lit
         the far corners of our
knowing, and which we never
         spoke of – observing
their passing in silence,
         those beacons breaching
our private zone of night;
         flashing like goonieman's
lanterns, some
         undeciphered code.
Only now I understand

         what spilled
                  from us then;
                           what spills, still.

MAREEL

for Cara

Mind that night in November, the pair of us
bursting from Mareel like late-comers
to the cinema-dark of the evening.

How we nearly missed it, the other show
that night: the aurora, the dancers, unspooling
their reels of green across the sky, despite

a bone-bright moon in the south. Mind
how the waves in Hay's Dock lit up with this
borrowed phosphorescence, and we skirled

at the spectacle of it all; a sky of light, a sea of sky,
and behind us, the noost of Mareel,
its north-pointed prow.

DE SELKIE STEPS

An here,

   de saat-shilled steps
   whaar I fan de selkie last year.

De sea widna hae her.
No lik yun:
   sweet-daed,
   eenless,
    lookin

   lik a daddit
   aald mön.

De uncan strange o it
   vexed me den.

   Whitna beak wid demmel foo
o eenwattir, but laeve
   her glunta-flesh

unspret?

Cassen awa
   apo de mairch
   o shoormal an stair,

THE SEAL STEPS

And here, the salt-bitten steps
where I found the seal last year.
The sea wouldn't have her. Not like that:
freshly dead, eyeless, looking like a washed-up old moon.
The strange spectacle of it distressed me then.
What beak would take its fill of eyewater,
but leave her lunar-flesh
unsplit?
Lost on the boundary of tidemark and stair,

halfgaets atween
        wan mirk
        an anidder.

Deday,
it's joost de steps
dat hadds.

Biggit fir a noost
            lang-akkered,
        dey lead me
tae dis mindin;

de blinnd o de ee,
de boady's draa.

halfway between one dark and another.
Today, it's just the steps that hold.
Built for a dock long-ruined,
they lead me to this memory;
the dim light of the eye asleep,
the body's beached mooring.

BLINND-MOORIE

de island

       koomed

wir braeth

       gied

lik ess

WHITE OUT

the island
burned to dust
our breath went
like ash before us

THE DIAGNOSIS

A rookery, long abandoned now,
had been built inside my body.

I don't know where the birds went
or why, one day, they uninhabited,

leaving only their barbed-wire
residues, strung across the boughs

of my hips; all sticks and spit,
all hollows meant for holding

something small, still desperately
alive. I'm sorry – I'm afraid

I know only my own dark canopy,
its filtering bones of light.

IX AND THE OCTOPUS

A dream with eyes open. It meant nothing.
Even then, I knew this. Still, I saw the octopus
that night, slung between the headboard

and the wall; a slow reaching for your body.
Nothing. I know this still. But even waking
will not slip the grip of seeing

how it sank that night into the seabed of your skin
and hung so prettily inside you, like a stomach
or a lung, or the dank cavity of a heart.

LAMPLICHT
24.06.16

a slundy o licht
sprickles

i de gaets made mirrors
fae dis drush,

an its lik we're staagin
abön some sukken,

sindered warld;
a cummelled city,

nönin de hushiebaa
o de raag,

whaar wir shadoos
best faa wis.

LAMPLIGHT

24.06.16

a swarm of light writhes on the pavements
made mirrors from this drizzle,
and it's like we're stalking above
some sunken, sundered world;
an upturned city, humming the lullaby of the rain,
where our shadows best become us.

DE SLOCKIT LICHT
for Adam

Mibbe it's dat mön i dy veins,
a lump i de blöd whit set du here,
ir mibbe du joost kent dis island
haads its wilt tings closs. Whitivver wye,

du seems tae fin dysel maist whaar de licht
is slockit: helliers, vodd hooses – du's taen
by de veesiks o dir stons, de wye a voice soonds
dere, fornenst de swaar o de dim.

THE SLOCKIT LIGHT

Maybe it's that moon in your veins;
a swell in the blood which sent you here,
or maybe you just knew this island holds
its lost things close. Whichever way,
you seem to find yourself most where the light
wrecks: sea caves, ruined houses –
you're taken by the folksongs of their stones,
the way a voice sounds there,
against the darkest point of the dark.

THE DARK ROOM

Your camera was not an eye.
It was a mouth.

AKKER

These days
I think more and more
about the tongue
of some ill-luckit
bog wife, weighed down

by ess and kleeber
in the helli-möld of her mouth,

and so perfectly preserved
you could trace the taste
of her own last supper,
catch the cadence
of her last word spoken –

a word
that I can never know
even if I'd heard it said,
her language
dead now;

     all akker,
         absence,

like how sea-glass
bears no mindin
of the bottle, nor the liquid
which it kept, the lips
that wrapped around its neck,

the message it once held
inside itself.

I thieve such pieces
on slockit days
when words leave me
at a loss, and all
near-hearted, present things
have sunk
into their darknesses;

in those smallest devastations
of the light,
I fear the silence
which the hills give back.

BARNACLE WING

We find it in the salt marsh:
           this single shock
    of goose wing

freshly
      torn

a soft cling
    of sinew at the absent body's
                join –

dropped like an arrow
    in the scrub;
            that way!

(But only the rooks
    out that way,
    only the sky numbing the hills.)

The wind coaxes
            feathers to a cruel muscle
      memory;
            tapered fingers crook, insist
                over there!
But *there's* nothing –
    only that blue bolt
    of sky, only the weight
    of corvid song

                  like hard water
                  on the tongue.

So where do we go from here?

                  Untethered as we are
We'll follow the wind
                       no doubt:

try to find some common language in it.

MIGRATION DAY

I had known this day was set in bone.
After all, that pull to North is hollowing me, too.
But now it's come, and all I think is *grief;*

this feels like grief. But it's not the flight
that can't be followed, this being left behind
that weighs on me. Something else

is in the fields now they've left us;
the marshes, bereft of them, are opening
again, like skin remembering

wounds. It's not enough to say
they will return. Something's always lost
in leaving. And anyway, I have less

faith in such assurances these days;
like when she said she did not fear her dying,
I knew she meant the indigo

of its moment – not the increments
of losing, not how each thing would slow
into its last. The day they left

was blue, and kind and sudden.
And still, some part of me
would beg them stay.

KOKKEL (N)

a compass; a lamp

[N. *kokle*]

SUMMER, 1939

I think of you sometimes – that other
granddaughter, with your islands now old
bedtime stories told in tall Marchmont rooms,
your darkness carved nightly into distance
and skerries. In the morning, gone.
The wynds of Edinburgh come to map
the secret patterns of your veins.

What bölliments of history make us who we are;
the summer of 1939, a telegram, a woman's choice
between the different weights of love. War made us
islands. Carved the shape of our distance out.
And though I doubt you think of me at all,
it's taken years for me to find

                              my way to you, to love
this city as I think you would. I've let the borders
of our separation wear thin, and sense you now
as that quiet crackling in the blood, like white noise,
or traffic, or the wind through trees, which sounds
so much like waves to me.

FOX

She sat so brazen
in the lovely blood
of the streetlamps

we thought, in our
old arrogance, that we
had imagined her

there – as if
we, who dare to call her *thief*,
could ever call her

likeness into being.
Her presence stilled us.
She did not look

our way, though she could
hear the weight of breath
in our lungs,

the absurd fanfare
of our bodies. I'm sure we
smelled of damage

long since done; all
oil and smoke unthreaded
by some distance,

something quelled
and dormant lingering
in our skin. But

this night was never
about us. We were nothing
but a minor intrusion

on her evening work.
She did not move when
we did. Beneath

her black gloves
the wet street glistened
like an altar.

She let us pass,
and we stole her image
in furtive glances.

A CARTOGRAPHY

You asked me once
where I thought 'the self' resides
inside the body – which dark,
red room we move in.

I mostly felt within my chest,
lodged between the ribcage
and the heart; a small fist, closed
around my own hot wires.

You said you felt most
behind your eyes. I liked that;
knowing I can see you lit
in your disquiet blue.

NIGHTWALK WITH NATTERJACKS

All around us the air
                ignites

on their staticky calls;
the lagoons become

        a lucky dip
of sex and spawn,

and we become more
             silhouette

        than substance;
something fit to enter

this shadowland
        of listening close,

        of hearing where
                our footsteps fall.

THE VANISHING MAP

That night you lay on the sofa of someone
else's living-room, the come-down settling
on you like the fuzzy leak of streetlights
through the blinds. You saw a map pinned
across the ceiling, and thought it clever: to see
the world as always upside down, like you
were a face on a playing card. Maybe you said this
out loud. Who knows. Of course, there was no

map there. You blinked and watched it sink
into white whorls of plaster; felt the horror
of that dissonance spread across your mind
like warm butter. You almost laughed. Trust
you to blink the world away like that; a ship
sunk, a lighthouse slockit, and you just lying
there with your eyes closed. You knew this time
it would not come back; no feckless faith
could ever raise your wrecks. Still, you tried.

ETYMOLOGY

listen
the wind through the trees
is naming this place

flickerings

THE MOTH TRAP

I never knew their marks
were just darker shades
of dust

that older mothwings fade
like pages

left opened   to the light

how in aging
they unknow themselves
shed this powder

of identity
grow soft into
                vanishings –

just imagine it:
all that residue

of you, wind-blown
through some flickering
wooded night

each mark
each word

                lifted

where all that's left   is flight –

HAIKU

I. HERMIT CRAB

a coiled house
slung like a creel on your back,
peerie kishie wife

II. LUKKIE MINIE'S OO

hanging out to dry
her threadbare delicates;
yun slut bog

III. VODD HOOSE

the wind still wants you;
I can hear its tongue testing
your crevices

IV. HAIRST

the scarecrow's pumpkin face
smiled at me last summer;
now he is sneering.

V. FIRST FROST, EDINBURGH

in the Links,
the palest skröf
of penicillin.

QUOYS, UNST

We came here
on the last day;
after the doontöm
which brought the earth
trötellin down the braes,
bringing to the halflight
all that we had hoped
would stay yirdit.

What took us
to this place of gaps,
whistling like the sibilants
of toothless bairns,
I still can't fathom;
but there was something
in its slow return to wilderness
which captured me.
And when I turned
to find you

                              gone,
I thought for a second
of that auld lore: of how,
perhaps, this place was built
on some long-abandoned knoll,
and in its fabled dark, I could be gone
a hundred years or more –

to emerge, then, from this absence
and hear your voice again,
I'd turn to ash.

SULLOM

and here lies
        the slow black pulse
                of the islands
which grew roads
        arterial, capillaries
across the map
                a slick spill of dark
        spinal fluid right

        down the middle.

In my memory it is lit
        as a magic lantern;
                all chatoyant glitter
        of another,
flickering world.
        City of the night,
                tucked in a far corner
        of my North –

a hologram,
        a mirknin heart.

PADDOCK STÖLS

Out here
is where the dirt
      is listening-in.

          Look,
            there!
Its white lugs
      pricked
and pointed;

      that fleshy nut
      of cochlea
          thrums.

RAIN GÖS

Du's surely ootdön,
sheerlin dy spos o rees
i dese doontöm days,

wi nane dat wants tae lö
fir dat sklent o urgent sang
dat first rivvined dy thrott.

Nivvir leet.
Dirs wadderheads i de aest;
sang ir silence, dir gadderin.

RAIN GOOSE

You're surely exhausted, singing
your prophecies of storms
in these downpour days,
with none who want to listen
for that long tear of urgent song
which first ripped open your throat.
Never heed. Columns of cloud are rising
in the east; song or silence, they gather.

OPHELIA
16.10.17

She arrives in a shroud threaded with desert,
smoke of forest fires in her hair. She kicks up
dust in the face of the sun, says 'Sweets, today
you can look that sky in the eye!' She kicks up
a fuss. Rolls away the stones that made tombs
of our mouths; turns light to pond water and water
to tonic. Ophelia is everyone's crazy Ex. A voice
rising in the leaves, chanting snatches of old lands
whose foundations are bone dust now. Hear her,
articulating our own secret knowledge: we
who lost the softest pieces of ourselves in the dark
red rooms. It was our story to carry. A quiet horror,
where a living thing once shivered. Ophelia's blown
those old feathers from the nest; scattered flowers
that fall like footsteps behind you on some autumn
night. You know the one; its moon smiling like a cut
in the open-wide mouth of the dark. She says tonight
is different: 'Haven't you heard, sweets? This old dark
was always ours for the taking. So we're taking it.
Tonight you'll walk home to the sound of your heart
beating in your head. For the first time, you'll hear it:
alive/alive/alive. Gosh, sweets. How it becomes you.'

SELKIE

Let us stop
at the moment of unsealing

the skin, the body within
slipping easily
from its heavy jacket of flesh

and into another kind
of heaviness.

Stop before
the story begins;

before the haafman
comes – moonstruck, monstrous –
to make his abduction.

There will be no need of forgiveness.
The hurt will not happen;

here
    the body

in whichever form it wants
will always belong
to itself.

Let us stop
at the moment's parting

poised
    between two vacant rooms

like blood moving
in the dual chambers
of the heart;   let us be

red, alive and undone
let us be barely human.

POEM NOTES

YURDEN

Text adapted from an old burial formula from the island of Yell. It appears to be written in a corrupted form of Danish, where the full text reads: Yurden du art fur af yurden du vis skav'd / Oktoa yurden nu ven dœd. / Op fra yurden skal du Opstaa, / naar Herren aar syne bastnan blaa. (*'Earth thou art for of earth thou wast made / to earth thou now returnest when dead. / From the earth thou shalt return, / when the Lord shall blow the last trumpet.'*)

HAAFMAN

The word 'lomm' here is from the haaf-language, which was used exclusively by fishermen out on the deep sea. It was believed by some that speaking words associated with the land would tempt severe misfortune; as such, certain words were swapped for ones deemed safe, usually drawn from the old Norn vocabulary.

SAAT I DE BLÖD

This was the first dialect poem I ever wrote. The words 'shoormal', 'mareel' and 'bonhoga' have cultural resonance here; *Shoormal* is the name of the first Shaetlan poetry collection I read, by Robert Alan Jamieson, 'Mareel' is the name of Shetland's first bespoke cinema and arts venue, and 'Bonhoga' is the name of an art gallery in the west side of the mainland.

RAAGA TREE
Quotation from 'Apo da Bloo Djoob' by Robert Alan Jamieson.

DE SLOCKIT LIGHT
A poem written for my friend Adam Howard, a folk musician who goes by the moniker The Duke of Norfolk. The poem takes its name from a slow air by Tom Anderson. When asked about the tune's inspiration, Anderson recounted that he was leaving his birth-home of Eshaness one January night in 1969, when he looked back and saw the lights of the houses going out one by one. Coupled with the recent death of his wife, the sight recalled to him the old word 'slockit,' meaning a light that has gone out.

RAIN GÖS
Lore around the red-throated diver suggests that it has the power to predict the weather, depending on the sound of its call and direction of its flight. 'Wadderheads' are a bank of clouds rising in columns or streaks on the horizon, which were also used in foretelling the weather, depending on which direction they lay: 'Nort-Sooth is a drooth – Aest-Wast fur a blast'.

QUOYS, UNST
In Unst, 'Quoys' is pronounced in the same way as the English word 'queues'.

ACKNOWLEDGEMENTS

I would like thank the following publishers, who first featured these poems: 'Haegri' and 'Moon Jellyfish' in the *Harlequin*; 'Saat i de Blöd' in *Northwords Now*; 'Mareel' in the *Reel to Rattling Reel* Anthology; 'Akker' in *Gutter*; 'Lamplicht' in *Bella Caledonia*; 'De Slockit Licht', 'Lamplicht', 'Akker' and 'Rain Gös' in the *Irish Pages*; 'Hairst' in *These Islands, We Sing* (Polygon, 2011) edited by Kevin MacNeil; 'Barnacle Wing' in *The Dark Horse*; 'The Moth Trap' in The Dark Mountain Project, and also runner-up in the 2018 Aesthetica Creative Writing Award; 'Haafman' and 'Speaking Shaetlan' in *The Edwin Morgan Sampler 2018*; 'Steepel' and 'Tirrick Skull' in the *New Shetlander*.

The following poems were written as part of a SGSAH RSPB funded artist-in-residency, at the Mersehead Nature Reserve in Dumfries and Galloway: 'Etymology'; 'Barnacle Wing'; 'The Moth Trap'; 'Migration' and 'Nightwalk with Natterjacks'.

The following poems, in various iterations, have taken form as filmpoems: 'Sullom'; 'The Oil Rigs'; 'Quoys, Unst'; 'Raaga' and 'Nightwalk with Natterjacks'
     To view these filmpoems and other work, please visit:
www.vimeo.com/roseannewatt

And thanks to the following people and organisations, whose support and encouragement over the years has meant everything: my parents Anne and Leslie, and my siblings, Alec, Eamonn and Jenny. For all the gifts you gave and continue to give me; my languages being the first.

Lexie and Alfie, for your stories and kindness.

Kevin MacNeil, for your endless generosity and wisdom, for showing me the best way to be a writer.

My poetry editor, Edward Crossan; I am so grateful that *Moder Dy* has found its home with Polygon.

My PhD supervisors, Kathleen Jamie and Sarah Neely.

My tutors at Stirling University: Scott Hames, Chris Powici, Paula Morris, Liam Murray Bell and Meaghan Delahunt.

The folk of Shetland's writing scene, with special thanks to Christine de Luca, Robert Alan Jamieson, Malachy Tallack, Mary Blance, Jen Hadfield, Ruth Mainland, Laureen Johnson, Brian Smith, Mark Ryan Smith, Jordan Ogg, Raman Mundair, Christie Williamson, Peter Ratter and Nat Hall.

My dearest heart, Stuart Thomson, and your incredible family: Lynn, Alec, Craig, Paul and Erin.

My beloved friends: Mhairi McNeill, Cara McDiarmid, Aidan Nicol, Chris Halcrow, Lorcan Henry, Claire Laurenson, Harry Whitham, Jenny Heubeck, Stephanie Wiseman, Kathy Hubbard, the Kermode-Williams family, Lucie Whitmore, Marjolein Robertson, Katya Moncrieff, Willem Cluness, Michael Watney and Hannah Tougher.

Shetland Arts, Maddrim Media, The Edwin Morgan Trust, SGSAH, *The New Shetlander*, Shetland ForWirds, Shetland Museum and Archives, An Lanntair, *The Island Review*.

GLOSSARY

aert:	earth
ahint:	behind
akker:	(1) fragments
	(2) ruin
biggit:	built
blinnd:	(n) a dim light; a short sleep
	(v) to close, as of the eyes
blinnd-moorie:	a snowstorm so severe it reduces visibility to zero
bloom:	the efflorescence on the outside of thoroughly dried fish
blue-finskit:	mouldy
bonhoga:	a spiritual or childhood place
bölliments:	odds and ends
bruks:	detritus
bu:	a house
cassen awa:	lost, generally at sea
cummel:	to turn upside down
daddit:	weary, worn out from overwork
deday:	today
demmel:	to fill a vessel by dipping it into water
dim:	dusk, twilight
djoob:	the deep sea (haaf language)

doontöm:	a heavy downpour
draa:	a place on the shore where a boat is drawn up
drush:	small fragments; a fine rain
ee:	eye
ert:	direction
ess:	ash, ashes
faa:	to fall; to become
fornenst:	against
gaet:	a path
glinks:	glints
gludderi:	watery and sunny, as of the sky in certain weathers
glunta:	the moon (haaf-language)
goonieman's lanterns:	small scrolls of birch bark which wash up on beaches and are known to burn well (also known as Loki's candles)
gru:	to smile with a threatening aspect
grün:	green
gurr:	mucous gathered in the corner of eyes
haafman:	a deep sea fisherman
hadd:	a nest; an animal's lair
hadds:	holds
haegri:	heron
hairst:	the harvest; work associated with that season

halfgaets:	halfway (literally 'halfpaths')
hame-trowe:	to return home; go homewards
hansel:	a gift, usually given to mark the beginning of something
hellier:	a sea cave
helli-möld:	burial ground (literally 'holy earth')
hintet:	spirited away
hushiebaa:	a lullaby
ill-luckit:	unlucky
innadaeks:	within the walls of the enclosure
kishie:	a woven basket
kist:	(1) a coffin (2) a chest or trunk
kleeber:	soapstone
knapp:	to speak in an affected manner, a Shetlander attempting to speak 'proper' English
koom:	to burn to dust
krub:	a small drystone enclosure for growing plants, especially kail; a small, walled garden
lapper:	(1) lapping gently (2) to congeal or curdle
leet:	heed
leid:	language
lift:	the sky

lisk:	wisp
lö:	to listen intently
lomm:	when the surface of the sea would grow light in colour as fish came below it (haaf language)
lukkie minnie's oo:	bogcotton
lump:	a tidal swell
mairch:	boundary mark
mareel:	phosphorescence on the water, especially in autumn
mindin:	memory; remembering
mirk:	dark
moorie-caavie:	a violent blizzard
nön:	to hum
noost:	the place, usually a hollow on the beach, where a boat is drawn up; a boatshed
ootadaeks:	outwith the enclosure; to be beyond the walls of the township (has metaphorical resonance with being out of place)
ootdön:	worn out
paddock stöl:	a mushroom
pining:	drying
raag:	a disreputable person; wet mist, almost a drizzle
ree:	a spell of stormy weather
reks:	to reach or stretch
rive:	to tear

röts:	roots
saat:	salt
sanna:	shall not
seems:	to notice
selkie:	(1) a seal
	(2) a mythical seal being, able to shed its skin and take human form on moonlit nights
shaipit:	shaped
shakkel:	entangle
sheave:	a slice, usually of bread
sheerlin:	singing, as of birdsong
shill:	to bite
shoormal:	the shoreline mark on a beach; the water's edge
sinder:	to sunder
skerry:	a rock standing out at sea
skirl:	to laugh or scream with a shrill sound
sklent:	a long tear
skröf	the surface layer; the surface of the sea
slockit:	extinguished, as of a light
slud:	an interval between showers
slundy:	a swarm
spo:	a prophecy
sprickle:	to wriggle or flounder
sprit:	to run very fast
staag:	to walk stiffly
starn:	a star

steepel:	a pile of fish on a beach, stacked crosswise to dry
stoor:	to stare in a dejected manner
strange:	wonder; amazement
sukken:	sunken
swaar:	the darkest point of the night
swart:	black
sweet:	fresh; lightly
tang:	seaweed, especially the kind which grows above the low-water mark
tattiebokey:	a scarecrow
thunderbolt:	a 'shetland knife', an ancient instrument, made of green porphyry
tirrick:	the Arctic tern
töm:	empty
tread:	thread
tröttel:	to mutter
twarter:	crossgrain
uncan:	strange
unspret:	unsplit
vaar:	to be wary; to be attentive to
vaege:	journey
veesik:	an old ballad or folksong
vex:	to be distressed
vodd:	vacated; empty; as a ruined house
wadderhead:	a pattern of clouds rising in columns or streaks on the

	horizon, used in forecasting weather
waak:	wake (as in a boat's wake)
wilt:	lost
yird/yirdit:	to bury/buried
yoal:	a six oared boat
yun:	that

SOURCES:

The Shetland Dictionary (Shetland Publishing Co, 1984) by John J. Graham; *Shetland Words* (The Shetland Times ltd, 2010) by A. & A. Christie Johnston; *A Shetland Glossary* (A. Gardner, 1914) by James Stout Angus; Wir Midder Tongue Facebook Group; orally sourced from family, friends and my own recollections.

MODER DY

You wake
in the afterlife

spit gravel
from your mouth,

like teeth
and cinders.

'Where am I?'
You think,

Somehow
you just know

it's almost
amniotic,

It makes you
feel calm,

this knowing
that isn't knowing.

surrounding you;
grey water,

wi dy kist
faan a yoal;

een gurry
wi saat an ess,

Dy first thowt
isna

'I ken dis pliss.'
Foo is dat?

fae de lapperin
o de wattir –

an uncan
hushiebaa.

dis mindin
dat isna mindin,

Du sits up
an sees de djoob

de sheave o waak
ahint dee

flat as a blade.
For the first time

        du seems dy haert
        geen still;

the heavy burden
of your body

        hintet. Whit is du,
        den? De thowt

unsettles you.
In the distance

        is an island, du kens
        du winna reach by

nightfall. You
settle for

        faeth alane.
        De gaet o sea gings on;

the darkness
quickening

        aroond dee is
        de start o starns.